A Hole In My Heart

Olayode Bada

A HOLE IN MY HEART

Olayode Bada © April 2021

ISBN: 979-874-643-385-5

Appreciation

To the Almighty God, my Creator and unto whom I shall return.

I equally appreciate my dear wife – Teju, 'Damilola, 'Tomisin, Adeola, Inioluwa, Ellen and Feranmi .

Characters

Durojaye	-	Adetutu's husband
Adetutu	-	Durojayse's wife
Ibukun	-	1st Child (Son)
Shade	-	2nd Child (Daughter)
Adelaja	-	3rd Child (Son)
Pastor		
Ajibola	-	Father of the new born baby
Treasure	-	New born baby girl
Mr. Simon	-	Neighbour
Johnson	-	Mr. Simon's Son
Mr. Dada	-	Neighbour
Attendant	-	Hospital Attendant
Doctor		
Nursing Officer		
Mich	-	Ibukun's friend and class mate
Mrs. Phillips	-	Ibukun's class teacher
Mrs. Eyitayo	-	Durojaye's cousin
Alhaji	-	Durojaye's Neighbour

Mr. Fredrick	-	Adelaja's teacher and mentor
Madam Jejelaye	-	Beer seller
Ponle	-	Adetutu's childhood friend
Neighbour 1	-	Sympathizer
Neighbour 2	-	"
Neighbour 3	-	"

ACT ONE SCENE ONE

Food is ready and has been placed on the dining table, covered with a piece of shawl while Durojaye is still dressing up in his room, preparing to go out to attend a function with his friends. Adetutu goes to look at the food again to be sure it has been properly served.

Adetutu: Shade, Shade.

[calls her daughter]

Shade: Yes Mummy

[She answers from her room and quickly runs to meet her mother standing near the dinning table on which the meal has been placed]

Adetutu: Can't you see that water has not been served here, ehn

Shade: I am sorry Mom, I will do just that right away.

[She immediately goes and returns with a jar of water from the refrigerator and places it on the table with a clean glass]

Shade: Water is here Mom

Adetutu: That's better. Your father isn't a Sparrow that will eat all the food without taking water and neither does he belong to the group often referred to as people that can eat even stones without taking water.

Shade: I have never said anything like that Mummy.

Adetutu: It's true you haven't but your action suggests something similar. In Africa, serving food without water implies the one to take the meal needs no water.

Shade: Alright Mom, it won't happen again.

Adetutu: Good.

[Adetutu and Shade both leave for Shade's room]

****

Durojaye gets to the table, adjusts the seat and sits to take his meal

Durojaye: *[starts taking the meal and he's very pleased with the taste, very delicious]* Mama Shade *[He calls]*

Adetutu: Yes my dear

[She emerges from Shade's room and moves towards him at the table]

Durojaye: Who prepares this meal?

Adetutu: *[Frowns immediately]* Is anything wrong with it again?

Durojaye: What have I said that suggests that something is wrong somewhere? I have sought to know who prepares the meal to commend his or her efforts, that's all.

Adetutu: Oh I am sorry. I didn't know that was what you meant. You know you complain about virtually everything and I just felt you were about doing what you know how to do best.

Durojaye: *[Now stops eating]* What do I know how to do best?

Adetutu: Complaints of course. Nothing, I mean nothing ever pleases you. You always see yourself as the only one that is right "Napoleon is always right"

[Frowns and turns away]

Durojaye: Anyway, let me just take the little I can before going out because if I should wait a little longer here maybe another problem may overtake my plan of going out.

[He resumes eating without any word further]

Adetutu: *[Hisses and leaves the scene]*

Durojaye: Only God knows the day I will begin to enjoy my home with this Devil called wife *[He says to himself]*

Adetutu: *[Resurfaces from only God knows where]* Yes, only God knows when you will begin to live like a man to be able to enjoy the Devil you call wife. Devil or not, I am your wife. You'd better let it register in your small brain and stop giving yourself unnecessary headache. A Cow doesn't value its' tail until it loses it.

Durojaye: That is the tail that does not add to the burdens of the Cow. You should have known by now that you are the only problem that I have, and the only source of all my worries.

Adetutu: I thought you said you have somewhere important going this morning. Why can't you just eat your food, go wherever you want and come back before toying with fire.

Durojaye: *[Remains mute as if he doesn't hear her 'cause he knows problem is already brewing]* Anyway thanks for the meal.

Adetutu: I don't have time for you. It's rather too early in the morning otherwise ….. Good for nothing husband.

Durojaye: Good for nothing or good for something, husband is husband either counterfeit or genuine.

[Shade in her room listening to the conversations between the duo]

Adetutu: Shade

Shade: Yes Mummy

[comes in looking sad]

Adetutu: You appear dull, what's the matter with you?

Shade: Mummy, both of you are the matter with me. I don't know when you people will begin to live together like other happy couples do. Daddy merely asked who prepared the meal and you answered him in such a rude manner.

Adetutu: Will you keep your dirty mouth shut? How dare talk to me like that, saying your own mother was rude.

Shade: Again am sorry Mom. I meant not to be rude. I only want to advise that you take things easy with Daddy. He isn't a bad person after all.

Adetutu: Just take care of the table. I know it's your mother that is a bad person. Isn't that what you are implying?

Shade: No ma, I haven't said that and never can I say that to my mother.

Adetutu: Just go to your room after taking care of the table. Like father like daughter.

[Hisses and leaves]

Shade: *[Soliloquizing]* One day you will understand my point and see reasons with me. *[Takes the dishes to the kitchen.]*

[Curtain falls]

ACT ONE SCENE TWO

Ibukun: *[Fetching water to fill the empty drums in the backyard]*

Shade *[He calls from the backyard]*

Shade: Yes brother

[She answers and goes to attend to him]

Ibukun: What have you been doing inside since, knowing that we have to fetch water this morning?

[He doesn't allow her respond before handing her his judgment]

A day will come that you avoid work like this and I will break this ugly head of yours.

Shade: You couldn't even wait to hear me out before passing this cruel judgment on me. Whatever happens, never you contemplate breaking my head – you hear? Your mind is always filled with evil thoughts. I haven't heard you for once think of something good or positive in your life. This is already telling on your studies if you don't know.

Ibukun: The day I will break this razor you call mouth, you will regret ever having me as your senior brother

Shade: Senior brother indeed with empty head.

Ibukun: Senior brother with blocked head you said?

Shade: No, not at all. Maybe you didn't hear me well.

Ibukun: What then did you say?

Shade: Empty head not blocked head.

Ibukun: What's the difference between six and half a dozen?

Shade: I don't know. Is this what you called me for?

Ibukun: No, I only wanted to know why you have not joined me in fetching water and also to let you know that the day I will descend on you, hmn, you will smell pepper.

Shade: Like mother like son. You look so much like Mummy in every way.

Ibukun: What do you mean?

Shade: Do you know that for a simple question asked by Daddy this morning, a big fight almost ensued if not for God's intervention and for Daddy's maturity. I don't know when you and Mummy will begin to do things right in this house so that we all can enjoy some peace that has always eluded us as a family. Remember Daddy comes home late not because of work or anything else but because of Mummy that is like a thorn in the flesh of the man.

The book of Genesis has it that the woman was taken out of the man but I wonder in this case if Mummy was ever taken out of Daddy because of their glaring incompatibilities. They are not in any way compatible.

Ibukun: *[Shows enthusiasm]* So Mummy and Daddy have performed their show this morning ehn. What a pity that I have missed the fun.

Shade: Do you call that fun?

Ibukun: What else do you want me to call a wrestling or boxing bout? Is Mike Tyson or Evander Holyfield not fighting to entertain the people and to make their Dollars? I enjoy watching Mummy and Daddy fight.

Shade: Why?

Ibukun: You know sometimes when watching interesting bouts on the Television, the Electricity Authority may decide to cut power but this one is live and direct, no power outage except for some uninvited Neighbours that always come to separate them.

Shade: I am so surprised at the kind of a child you are to our parents. I wonder if any reasonable child could ever say a thing like this about his or her parents.

Ibukun: Have I said anything that is out of place? I have only said what I know and of course what I see everyday. Aren't you too a living witness?

Shade: Enough of all these dirty words. I have to leave at once if you don't have anything reasonable you have called me for.

[Shade looks at him with pity, hisses, shakes her head and leaves while he continues fetching water]

[Curtain falls]

ACT ONE SCENE THREE

(Durojaye has gone to attend the naming ceremony of a child that a family has just been blessed with. The couple has been married for a number of years without the fruit of the womb. They are happy and grateful to God who has blessed them with a bouncing baby girl)

Pastor: *[Standing to give the names of the child]*

Before I go ahead to pronounce the names of this beautiful child which I expect you all to say after me as I mention them, allow me to lead you into the word of God first. I won't take much of your time. *[As the Pastor begins his speech, the baby starts crying for food]*

You know it's for this we're here gathered and we have all been enjoying ourselves, so, we mustn't allow her go hungry while we're satisfied.

[Laughter by all. He beckons on the mother to carry the baby so as to feed her with breast milk; the very best for infants according to research findings]

Pastor: *[Now continues with his message from the Holy Book]*

According to Psalm 127 verses 3, 4 and 5. Lo, children are an heritage of the Lord; and the fruit of the womb is his reward. As arrows are in the hand of a mighty man; so are children of the youth. Happy is the man that have his quiver full of them: they shall not be ashamed, but they shall speak with the enemies in the gate. In summary, for what is contained in those verses to be achievable, Husbands, love your wives and you wives must be submissive to your husbands. Whatsoever the wife does, the husband must learn to endure and always try to forgive her knowing that they are both not of the same family background. Wherever there are cracks in your families you men here present, please go back home and make amends.

'Shout hallelujah somebody'

[All chorus a loud hallelujah after which he begins to mention the names of the baby as contained in the paper handed over by the baby girl's father .As the Pastor call the names, the people present chorus the names after him. Durojaye has been carried away by the message of the man of God. He thinks of what

to do and how to fix the problems he has always been having with his wife. He loves her but she is a thorn in his flesh]

Before we all pray for the child, I like to ask some of you to mention the names we have just given this precious and perfect gift of God.

[As the usual practice of Ministers of God, the Pastor points to Durojaye to mention one of the names of the baby girl]

Durojaye: *[Stands up, pauses for a while as all the people focus attention on him and then gently says Adetutu. There is outburst of laughter as he couldn't mention one correct name of the baby girl. He's busy thinking of how to make amicable settlement with his wife]*

Pastor: It could be that he wants to add yet another name to the already long list of names. God bless you sir as you have your seat.

[Others begin to mention the names one after the other while the Pastor rounds it off by saying the closing prayer]

Ajibola: *[Gives the vote of thanks on behalf of the family including Treasure – the new child]*

On behalf of my dear wife and Treasure our baby, I say a big thank you to all of you that find the time to grace this occasion. May God bless you all.

ACT ONE SCENE FOUR

[Durojaye on his way home thinking of what strategy to adopt to get his wife reason with him to put an end to the incessant fight in the family]

Knock on the door.

Shade: Who's there?

Durojaye: It's me

Shade: *[Peeps through the window]*

Ah Daddy, welcome sir

[opens quickly to let him in, she is happy to see him return home early]

How was the occasion Daddy?

Durojaye: Beautiful and full of valuable lessons to learn.

Shade: *[Curious to know what he meant]* What sort of lessons Dad?

Durojaye: How I wish your mother was there, we were taught how to make our family life happy. We were told to always give peace a chance in our homes no matter what, and to love one another. I realize there can't be any meaningful or appreciable developments in a family where there is rancor. All of us know we have not been enjoying peace in this family. *[At this point Adetutu emerges from her room, upon seeing her, Durojaye stretches his hands forward to embrace her]*

Durojaye: How are you d-a-r-l-i-n-g

Adetutu: You should know without asking. I heard all you have been telling your daughter. You wished I went with you to where I wasn't invited. Oh did you invite me?

Durojaye: Look dear, I have not said anything bad against you. I only wanted you to be ....

Adetutu: Just hold it. You wished I was there to hear by myself. What are you insinuating? That I am the trouble shooter in this house ehn, I see, Mr. Innocent. If care is not taken, I will give more than double what you have bargained for this afternoon.

Shade: Mummy, Mummy. Why is it that you're always on Daddy's throat? He hasn't said anything bad about you. He was only trying to ....

Adetutu: *[cuts her short]*

Will you shut up your dirty mouth? What is this world turning to? When did it become an acceptable habit in Africa for children to be participating in the discussions of elders. This world has really turned to something else.

Shade: Mummy, I am indeed very sorry. Elders are not just talking here but are quarreling and this is what Daddy is just saying that we needed peace in this family and I must tell you today that you are the one that has not been allowing that to happen.

Adetutu: *[Using her left fore finger to cross Shade's mouth while using her right hand to show her the way to go immediately]*

Keep your mouth shut little rat and get yourself out of here this minute.

Shade: *[Not happy at her Mother's behavior, quietly goes into her room]*

Why is Mummy always doing this to Daddy *[She says to herself]*

Durojaye: Adetutu! Adetutu!! Adetutu!!!. How many times did I call you?

Adetutu: Sorry I didn't count

Durojaye: Three times. It could be that your memory is failing

Adetutu: What's the matter this time? *[Frowning and hissing]*

Durojaye: I just want to beg you to please forgive me if there's any way I have wronged you. You see, I don't want the people around to be hearing bad news about us anymore. All these fights have to stop and we must try to live in peace henceforth. I therefore want you to join hands with me to ensure this. Darling, I have forgiven you all that you have ever done to me in the past and I want to assure you that I am not keeping any record of your wrong doings. Please let us start on a clean slate now and our family will be better for it.

Adetutu: I will join hands with you provided you make your hands available.

Durojaye: I promise not to do anything to jeopardise this agreement

Adetutu: Look here, I have not and I am not entering into any agreement with you. Did you see me sign any document to be of good conduct when I am not a school girl? All I have said is that I will cooperate with you to ensure that peace reigns supreme in this family provided you create the enabling environment.

Durojaye: Anything you want me to do I will. Thank you dear for this assurance.

[Shade eavesdropping in her room is very happy with the agreement reached by the two feuding parties but she's in doubt if it could last because her mother is sure to breach it in no distant time]

Durojaye: *[Smiling and trying to put his hands around her neck]*

Now what about the next item on the list?

Adetutu: Which list and what item are you talking about?

Durojaye: When a man leaves home and returns much later, you ask if he cares for water and possibly food. You also enquire about where he has been. All of these make him to know that you truly care about him and he will be so happy to hear that.

Adetutu: My dear don't worry. You know we have just reached a consensus. So when next you go out, you will be treated as such on your return. Would you like to go somewhere else again to return later to qualify for a glass of water?

Durojaye: I don't need to go anywhere I do not intend only to earn me a glass of water, so, you can keep your glass.

[Adetutu claps and laughs, then goes into the kitchen]

ACT TWO SCENE ONE

[Durojaye goes to the small garden at the backyard to have a look at the few crops planted there]

Durojaye: *[Hears a voice demanding to see him]*

S-h-a-d-e *[He calls to know who is asking of him]*

Shade: Yes Daddy

[She comes not looking so happy]

Durojaye: What is the matter with you and who is asking of me?

Shade: Daddy, it's Mr. Simon our neighbor Sir

Durojaye: Oh that's right. Where is he?

Shade: In the living room Sir.

Durojaye: Hope there's no problem

Shade: No Sir except that he has come to report Ibukun

Durojaye: What about?

Shade: Ibukun beat up his son when fetching water this morning while you were away

Durojaye: Really? Let me see him at once

[He quickly goes in to attend to him. Good day Sir. He greets]

Mr. Simon: You're welcome Sir. How is the weekend?

Durojaye: Fine. I went to attend the naming ceremony of a child in the morning

Mr. Simon: I guessed as much. I told my wife you must gone out by then. *[Sits properly]*

Durojaye: I went out just immediately after my breakfast

Mr. Simon: Ibukun beats Johnson blue black this morning when they were both fetching water. In order not to create disaffection between us, he came to report the matter but instead for your wife to plead with the two boys encouraging them not to fight again, she blamed Johnson and told him to learn to respect Ibukun because they are not mates. Johnson was annoyed the more but I told not to worry that I will see you. Please Sir, caution Ibukun and tell your wife to learn how to deal with issues involving these young ones. I know if he had met you, you would have pleaded with the two of them.

Durojaye: I thank you for this beautiful step you have taken. We are one and nothing must divide us. I promise to talk to both of them. Please appeal to Johnson on my behalf although I'll still see him. Let me say it again that nothing must come in between us.

Mr. Simon: I have always known you to be a nice person. I promise that we will continue to live together in peace. Thank you.

[Mr. Simon rises to leave while Durojaye is about opening the main door for his exit]

Adetutu: Good day Sir

[She greets as she emerges from one of the rooms]

Mr. Simon: You are welcome ma

Adetutu: Please sir, warn your son. I learnt he was rude to my son this morning just because he went to fetch water in your compound. If he doesn't want us to fetch water from your compound any more then we turn elsewhere.

[As Mr. Simon is to respond, Durojaye prevents him by responding first]

Durojaye: Is this the best way to handle issues between two children, are these little ones not one, why have you chosen to talk this way, can two wrongs make a right?

[Turning to Mr. Simon] Please Sir don't feel offended and if you do, just take it that I am the one who has offended you and *[bending down as if prostrating]* I beg for you pardon.

Adetutu: Shameless husband, prostrating for his mate over what? Ordinary water. Any lazy and poor man that can't afford to put water in his compound must always continue to prostrate for his mates even his juniors for his family to get water. *[Mr. Simon couldn't say a word other than leaving at once because it could degenerate to pouring of hot water on him if he fails to leave on time].*

Mr. Simon: Thank you and bye

Durojaye: Thank you too

[Mr. Simon leaves hurriedly and the door was shut after him]

Adetutu: Durojaye or what do you call yourself. You know I have always been saying that you are not a man. How could your mate have the effrontery to come into your own house to report your son and the only thing you could do is to start begging. What did he accuse your son of, did he come with Police men and why can't you for once stand up, beat your chest and talk like a man? I am beginning to regret the day I gave you my hand in marriage without knowing how cowardly you could be - what a weakling. I just pray we don't have any serious problem, from the look of things, you will deny us. Your denial will be far greater than that of the Saviour by Peter three times just because a small girl asked him if he belong to the camp of his master. I am sure if he was asked by huge man, or an armed person, he would deny his master a dozen and a half times.

Durojaye: Adetutu remember it was just this afternoon I pleaded with you on the need to allow peace reign in this house and you promised. Let me ask if what you have done now is not a breach of that agreement. Let's try as much as we can to be at peace with ourselves and every other person around us. I know you're a nice woman, you go to Church regularly and you study the Bible too if not, you would not have known how Peter denied ever having anything to do with his master but remember that it is said in the Epistle of Paul the Apostle to the Romans, chapter twelve verse eighteen that if it is possible, as much as depends on you, live peaceably with all men. You see my dear, all men here refer to everyone, your neighbours inclusive.

Adetutu: Thank you Mr. Ecclesiastes the Preacher. Don't forget that many wars were in the Old Testament days of the same Book. Are you saying those people were wrong by going to war instead of being at peace with everyone? Anyway I have heard you and you too must hear me by providing enough for your family so we can stop begging for essentials of life like water.

[She dashes away without waiting for further response from her husband]

Durojaye: Shade *[He calls]*

Shade: Yes Daddy *[She comes to her father]*

Durojaye: Where is Ibukun the boxer or should I call him the wrestler or better still the Tiger?

Shade: He has gone to the field to play Football

Durojaye: Did you see him going?

Shade: Yes I did. He went in company of Johnson and one other boy; the three of them wen together.

Durojaye: Can you see the innocence of these small children, playing together after the fight they had in the morning and yet a mother – an adult – is trying to create further problems out of the said fight when the children themselves have since put all of that behind them.

Durojaye: Darling *[He calls to explain a few things]*

Adetutu: Yes I am here. Has anybody come to make yet another report and this time what about? *[Standing akimbo with her hands on her waist]*

Durojaye: Can't I call you for once without you saying these annoying words after you have just promised to make for peace in this house and to be of better behavior. *[Talking in high tone]*

Adetutu: I am sorry my dear – Mr. Peace maker, now what's the matter?

Durojaye: We needed to be more careful the way we handle issues of life. The two children that fought in the morning have both gone to the field to play football. What I want you to know is that we mustn't allow any issue with these children cause rancor between us and others around.

Adetutu: Thank you again. I am beginning to enjoy your sermons, not on the Mount this time but in the room. When will you be ordained?

Durojaye: Ordained as what?

Adetutu: Priest of course and then I will become a Reverend Mrs.

[Both laugh]

ACT TWO SCENE TWO

[In the evening after the return of Ibukun from the football field, his father calls to admonish him]

Durojaye: Where have you been?

Ibukun: Backyard Sir

Durojaye: Doing what?

Ibukun: Washing my boxers' knicker

Durojaye: It's better you are washing boxers' knicker and why not Wrestlers' knicker? I learnt fought Johnson in the morning; when did you become a boxer? I don't want you to take after your mother who fights everyone that comes her way. In fact I am earnestly praying for her to see the need for her to drop all these bad attitudes of hers. I know you have already taken after her but I want you to change as this may affect you in the future if you continue to fight everyone around just like your mother.

Ibukun: I promise to be a good boy daddy.

Durojaye: It is everyday you promise to be of a good boy yet you get worse by the day. Let me tell you that I am already getting worried about your way of life. With the way you're carrying on with life, your future seems bleak. At your age, you have learnt how to leave home without getting to school. You have known how to steal money and spend it all before returning home and you are my first child, my very first seed; what kind of foundation are you laying for your younger ones

Ibukun: Daddy I said I am sorry and that it won't repeat itself.

[Durojaye continues talking to register his displeasure]

I don't know how many times I have said am sorry and you're still talking; what else do you want me to say sir?

Durojaye: Are you asking me that question?

Adetutu: *[Comes from the kitchen]*

Don't put words into my son's mouth. He has said times without number that he is sorry. What else do you want to hear from him? May I tell you not to create unnecessary fears in him. Don't make him the kind of man you are that you cannot for once assert yourself, speak and do things like a man. My own son must not take after a coward father.

Durojaye: Woman, enough of these stupid talks. Who invites you to this matter in the first place?

Adetutu: Must I wait to be invited before correcting a bad idea of yours. Aren't you my husband and is he no longer my son?

Durojaye: You had better learn not to intrude again and stop bothering yourself with things that do not concern you.

Adetutu: *[Laughs loud and long]*

So my son's issue does not concern me. *[Laughter]* If my son's issue is none of my business please tell me sir whose issue should be of concern to me. You good for nothing coward *[Pointing her finger at him touching his nose]*

Durojaye: Are you not over-stepping your bounds woman, you devil called wife.

Adetutu: Who is over-stepping her bounds? *[She removes her head tie and fastens it round her waist in readiness for a showdown]*

Durojaye: Just allow peace to reign in this house today. You are always looking for an opportunity to fight and that is not good enough

Adetutu: You have to show me or teach me that which is good enough. Bastard called husband.

Durojaye: Who is the bastard, you or i?

Adetutu: That question is not for me but for your people at home.

Durojaye: Are you referring to my parents woman?

Adetutu: Whoever that is there. Just go and ask them

[Durojaye turns to leave the scene, she pulls him back, falls down and gets annoyed]

Durojaye: *[Rises up]* What's the matter with you?

Adetutu: I don't know what the matter with you is

Durojaye: *[Moves closer and gave her a slap on the cheek]*

Are you out of your mind?

Adetutu: Whether I am out of my mind or not you will know and today you must kill me.

Durojaye: I am not a killer, so, I won't kill you. I will only teach you the lesson you needed to learn since you were not properly brought up by your parents or maybe you were the one that refused your parents' instructions.

[As they are fighting, neighbours rush in to separate them. He has already taught her a lesson she won't forget in a hurry as she already has swollen face as a result of heavy punches]

Mr. Dada: What is the matter again this evening?

Durojaye: Sir, she is the cause of all these. She is too stubborn and would never take to correction. She provoked me beyond what I could bear. Everyone has his or her elastic limits. I never intended touching her but she made me to do against my wish. I am sorry.

Mr. Dada: Just take it easy. Learn to control your temperaments under any circumstance. You are a man and must always see yourself as one and act same.

Durojaye: Thank you sir.

Mr. Dada: You can see she's groaning in pains and crying like a baby so please go and comfort her and tell her it wasn't intentional.

Durojaye: Thank you sir. I will do that.

Curtain falls

ACT TWO SCENE THREE

[Adetutu wakes up early to prepare food for the children who would be going to school. She is feeling dizzy]

Adetutu: *[Soliloquizing]*

What could have been responsible for this dizziness this morning, could it that I didn't sleep well enough.

Shade, Sh-aa-de *[she calls]*

Shade: *[Wakes from her sleep and goes to the kitchen to meet her mother]*

Yes Mummy

Adetutu: *[Starring at her without a word]*

Shade: Mummy, you called me

Adetutu: Yes I did but won't you greet first before asking why I have called you.

Shade: I am very sorry Mom *[She kneels down and greets]*

Adetutu: Good morning to you too, hope you slept well.

Shade: Yes ma.

Adetutu: Good. I am not feeling well this morning and I don't know what the issue is; so, you're to finish the food preparation. There's yam in the pot on the Stove; all you needed to do whenever it's ready is just to fry Eggs so that you can eat before going to school.

[She goes back to her room and lies on the bed]

Durojaye: Why are you in bed again?

Adetutu: I am feeling dizzy and I don't know what's wrong. It's as if I am feeling some general weakness of the body.

Durojaye: Maybe you needed to reach for Analgesics immediately after you must have eaten.

Adetutu: Analgesics are not antidotes for eye problems. I said I am feeling dizzy can't you understand?

Durojaye: Yes you're right but the weakness could be responsible for the dizziness I guess.

Adetutu: Oh Chief Medical Director. You are talking as if you ever had a Medical Practitioner in your family.

Durojaye: You and the sharp razor you call your mouth. Even when you're not feeling well, your razor is still as sharp as if nothing is wrong with you. Whether we have Doctors in our family or not, just take drugs that will relieve you of all that you have complained.

Adetutu: Thanks for your care Mr. Caring husband.

[He leaves the room to get some drugs for her use. He later returns with some drugs with instructions on usage]

Durojaye: *[In the room again]*

How are you now

Adetutu: Better

Durojaye: Have you eaten?

Adetutu: Yes, but just a little.

Durojaye: Please try and take some more. I've got some drugs that are better taken after meals.

Adetutu: Thanks for your kindness. Don't you know that self – medication is bad? After all, you're not a Medical person; why must you just go to a roadside medicine dealer to procure drugs to treat what hasn't been properly diagnosed by a competent medical practitioner

Durojaye: Are you saying what I have done is bad?

Adetutu: No, no, no. Don't misunderstand me at all. What 'am saying is that it is risky and therefore not good for anyone to go to those boys selling drugs on the streets to buy drugs to be administered on patients that have not been seen by Doctors, examined and for drugs to be prescribed appropriately.

Durojaye: I won't do that again. I admit I have done this in error.

Adetutu: Let me get prepared so that we can go and see the Doctor at once.

Durojaye: *[Pointing to the drugs]*

What happens to these ones?

Adetutu: I don't know. All I know is that I am not going to touch them not to talk of taking them. Many have lost their lives due to this type of ignorance. The most appropriate thing to do is to consult the Doctor any time anyone is ill. The people must not even wait until they take ill before going for routine medical checkup to ascertain their fitness or wellness and whenever anything bad is about coming up, such can nipped at the bud.

[She gets dressed up and both are ready for the hospital]

Adetutu: Did you remember to give the children money for Snacks when they were leaving for School?

Durojaye: You worry unnecessarily over everything. What gives you the impression that I must have forgotten? I made sure they left nothing behind.

Adetutu: Now let's go and don't forget that we're not going to that medicine store on the second street.

Durojaye: Meaning what?

Adetutu: That you have to go with enough money. We may be asked to do some tests before buying the drugs that may be prescribed eventually.

Durojaye: Don't worry. God is in control.

Adetutu: I know God is in control and will forever be. All I am asking is for you to play your own part well by going with enough money, leaving God to play His own part which He has always been playing effectively well. Remember God will not play your own part for you.

[Both leave for the hospital]

ACT TWO SCENE FOUR

[At the Out Patient Department, Patients sit in rows waiting to see the Doctors in order of their arrivals]

Durojaye: Don't worry my dear, it will be our turn.

Adetutu: Thank you. I don't have any other option so why do I have to worry at all, after all I suggested coming here. Left to you, it would have been from one medicine dealer to another on the streets.

Durojaye: Remember we're not at home. We don't need to be washing our dirty linen in the open stream.

Adetutu: I don't care where you wash your linen, the most important thing here is for the linen to be clean. What is bad is bad and must not be encouraged. Period.

Durojaye: Thank you

[A Ward Attendant comes in with some cards on her hands ready to make some announcements]

Attendant: Good morning to you all; please listen attentively to your names. If your name is mentioned, please go to that room and be on the seats provided, a Doctor will attend to you there.

Doctor: Good morning madam

Adetutu: Good morning Doctor.

Doctor: Who is this?

[Pointing to her husband]

Adetutu: My husband Sir.

Doctor: That's right. It is good for men to assist their wives even to the hospital, not abandoning them.

Durojaye: Thank you sir.

Doctor: What's the matter madam?

Adetutu: I don't know and that's why we're here

Doctor: Do you mean you don't know what has brought you here?

Adetutu: If I know, I won't be here Doctor. You see I am feeling dizzy and I want you to tell us what is wrong.

Doctor: That is what I mean. I simply want you to tell me how you are feeling, this will enable me know exactly what to do for you. Doctors are not God to know everything without being informed.

[She explains to him and he goes through the report of the vital signs carried out by the Nursing Officer]

Doctor: *[Fills a small form demanding pregnancy test be carried out; gives her the form and instructs her to go give it to the Nursing*

Officer and to take further instructions from her]

Adetutu & Durojaye: Thank you Doctor.

Doctor: Please do the test on time and come back with the result

[They both leave the consulting room]

Nursing Officer: *[Collects the form, reads through and instructs a Ward Attendant to lead them to the Laboratory department]*

Madam, The Doctor has recommended pregnancy test. This woman *[pointing to the Ward Attendant]* will lead you to where to go for the test but make sure to come back with the result to see the Doctor again.

Adetutu: Thank you ma

[After the payment of some prescribed fees at the Laboratory, she gets a small specimen bottle for urine sample which must be early morning urine taken before food or water. The next day she comes with it and was confirmed to be pregnant]

******

[Back home]

Durojaye: How was the place?

Adetutu: Your Messenger has delivered the message.

Durojaye: What are you saying, I can't understand.

I said how about the Laboratory test?

Adetutu: And I said your Mail has been signed, sealed and delivered.

Durojaye: Why can't you be serious for a moment?

Adetutu: Now that you still feign ignorance let me tell you, I am pregnant.

[He is not happy at the news considering the additional financial burden on him]

Durojaye: So you're pregnant now.

Adetutu: I know I am not married to a husband that is deaf and dumb and I am sure you heard me right' I am pregnant, period

[He manages to say congratulations but not from the bottom of his heart]

Durojaye: Were you given drugs, have you started taking them and how soon will you start the Ante- Natal Clinic?

Adetutu: You ask too many questions at a time. Are you a Lawyer carrying out cross-examination, even if you are, I am not an accused person and neither am I in the dock. To please you, I was given drugs, I am yet to commence administering them and the Ante Natal Clinic is to begin soon. Are you now satisfied Mr. Expectant Father?

Durojaye: What else do you want me to say. As much as I care for you and as much as I show you love, it has always been hatred in return. How I wish you could one day behave like a loving and responsible wife.

Adetutu: You can go ahead and continue to say all manner of things. I don't just have time for you now. I should have returned from the market by now if not for the hospital I went.

Durojaye: Do you still want to go to the market? Don't forget it's mid-day already and it is scorchingly hot out there.

Adetutu: It is not compulsory I go provided you are ready to go to bed with an empty stomach.

Durojaye: Why does anybody have to go to bed hungry?

Adetutu: I know you will shout at that. Your pains threshold is much lower than that of even these children. Without food, I know you will just lie down counting the Nails on the ceiling without sleep till day break.

Durojaye: Are you taking me for a baby?

Adetutu: No, worse than a baby. A baby is better than you whenever hunger strikes you. I don't know why a man like you cannot hold himself together when hungry. You will then be shivering like one ready to sell his birthright for a morsel of pottage.

Durojaye: Thank you for painting me in the colour that is not mine or dressing me in a borrowed robe.

Adetutu: I hope you haven't forgotten so soon that from the very first day of conception to delivery, expectant mothers require funding, I mean good funding.

Durojaye: How can I forget when this is not our first time. I think the funding isn't immediate because I am not financially alright now.

Adetutu: You are not buoyant yet you keep knocking at my door all the time. Let me remind you in case you have forgotten that I needed to register immediately for Ante-Natal Care. After the booking, I have to be visiting the hospital on my clinic days and don't forget also that the routine haematinics and so on are not free of charge. It is only the exercises we do and the songs we sing that are free. If some governments have their ways, they may be surcharging us for the choruses we render on our clinic days but thank God we don't pay for the songs, they are rendered free.

Durojaye: I will make some money available later today to take of the booking a few other things.

Adetutu: O.K. Sir Mr. Expectant Father.

[Knocks on the door]

Durojaye: Hello, who's at the door?

Ibukun: It's me

[Enters and greets]

Durojaye: Welcome. What is the matter with you and why is your uniform torn as much as this?

Ibukun: I was beaten by that wicked teacher of ours.

Durojaye: Did he beat every other person in your class?

Ibukun: No Sir, I was the only one.

Durojaye: What did you do to have deserved the teacher's cane?

Ibukun: I don't know. I don't know why the man just don't like my face. He doesn't like me a bit.

Adetutu: Ibk *[As Ibukun is fondly called]*

What did just say? How on earth is a teacher supposed to have beaten a child this way regardless of the magnitude of the offence the child must have committed.

Papa Ibk *[calling her husband]*, what is the next step to take now. Let's go at once to that School to teach the stupid teacher the lesson of his life.

[Ibukun happy at his mother's reaction]

Durojaye: We cannot just do that. Let us wait for his sister's return. She may have a completely different story to tell.

Adetutu: Are you saying that my child is lying? How can someone beat your child to a pulp like this and you're still here waiting and thinking not knowing what to do.

[Shade knocks and enters]

Shade: Good day Daddy and Mummy.

Adetutu: How are you my daughter and welcome.

Shade: Has Ibk told you what he did at School today?

Adetutu: What he did or the bad treatment given him by that ugly teacher.

Shade: I don't understand what you are talking about.

Adetutu: Then tell me what happened

Shade: Ibk stole someone's money and was discovered. He still went ahead to beat the boy for reporting the matter to the Authority. He was brought out in the assembly and given some strokes of the cane.

Adetutu: How much did he steal for him to have been beaten this way? I have to be at the School tomorrow.

Shade: Either you or Daddy has to be in the School tomorrow. He was told to bring his parents tomorrow. They said he might be suspended from School if his parents fail to show up.

Adetutu: Is it as serious as that?

Shade: Yes. It is almost every day that his fellow students report him to the School Authority for one offence or the other.

Durojaye: Can you now see one of the reasons why I said we needed to find out exactly what has happened.

Adetutu: Are you saying all that Shade has said could be true?

Durojaye: Shade is not an outsider. She's a member of this family. How can she be telling lies against her own brother even in his presence? You are spoiling this the more. Remember you're not helping him in any way. This boy is already a spoilt child and you are responsible for his moral decadence.

Adetutu: I know this is what you will say. Whenever a child is doing well, the glory goes to his father but the moment the child behaves otherwise, the mother takes responsibility. Tomorrow is just around the corner that I will have to see his teacher and warn him sternly never to beat my child this way again or else ....

Durojaye: Or else what?

Adetutu: You just wait and see. It is said that what a man hopes to name his child is better kept to his chest.

Durojaye: Keep whatever you like to your chest; that is your own kettle of tea and not mine.

ACT THREE SCENE ONE

Adetutu: Good morning *[She greets her husband]*

Durojaye: Good morning and how are you

Adetutu: Fine and you?

Durojaye: We give God all the glory

Adetutu: Hope you remember we're going to Ibk's School this morning

Durojaye: To do what if I may ask?

Adetutu: To meet his teacher of course. Is your memory failing so fast, have you forgotten we were both informed yesterday that our attention is needed today at the School?

Durojaye: I see. What time do you want us to be there?

Adetutu: As soon as possible.

Durojaye: You mean even before the arrival of both the staff and students?

Adetutu: How can you be talking like this?

Durojaye: How are my talking, don't you know it's a shameful thing to be invited this way? It shows our son isn't brought up properly which may be responsible for his misbehavior; this is an indictment on our part as parents. I will advise you join hands with me to give this boy good upbringing to guarantee better future.

Adetutu: Who says he's not well brought up, you or the teacher? If you know this is what you are going there for, you better stay back and allow me handle the issue myself. Good or bad, my child is my child.

[The children leave for School with a message for the teacher that his parent will be there]

Mich: *[Ibukun's School mate living nearby, walking abreast with him to School]*

Good morning Ibk.

Ibukun: Good morning and how are you?

Mich: I am fine. Did you remember to invite your parents?

Ibukun: Yes I did. My mother will come later.

Mich: What about your father?

Ibukun: I don't know.

Mich: Try and be a good boy please. I love you I don't like the way you behave. I know you can still turn a new leaf.

Ibukun: Yes I will. Thank you.

Mich: Have you done your assignment?

Ibukun: Which one?

Mich: Mathematics' assignment

Ibukun: *[Laughs]* You know our teacher is not serious

Mich: Why

Ibukun: He says we should solve a linear equation

Mich: Is that what makes him unserious?

Ibukun: Yes. What is the meaning of this jargon;

$5(x+2) -3(x-5)=1$. Find x; When he knows already that everything equals 1, why is he asking us to solve the equation; don't you agree too that he's not serious

Mich: Ibukun, you're not getting it right.

Ibukun: What is it that I'm not getting right? It is the teacher that is getting it wrong. Let us discuss better things and not that useless man that calls himself our Mathematics teacher.

Mich: Do you know that the people are noticing that you are refusing learning. Let me tell you that Education is simply the best and the surest key to success or greatness in life. It is better you handle it with all the seriousness it requires.

Ibukun: Thank you, I will advise that you pursue a career that will make you end up a preacher; if you are lucky, you may become of these General Overseers.

Mich: That is not the point.

Ibukun: Point or no point, the job of the General Overseer is one of the most lucrative around town. It is even better than working in Oil companies. The only job that compares with it in Africa is Politics. The Politicians are fantastically corrupt while the General Overseers no longer ride Jeeps but Jets; as it is now evangelism in the air. How I wish I have their kind of talent.

Mich: If you study hard, you too can own a Jet.

Ibukun: That's true but certainly not as easy as that of a G.O. All you needed to do first is to and learn how to speak good English, study the Holy Book a little bit, then take a loan to make your Sanctuary quite attractive, then you have arrived.

[As they talk and walk along, the School bell rings]

Mich: That's the School bell; we will soon be late, let's run

Ibukun: No, I cannot run. Why do I need to start running when nobody or nothing is chasing me and I am not chasing anything or anybody either.

Mich: Then I have to leave you alone.

[Ibukun gets to School late, joins the other late comers in kneeling down]

Ibukun: I am just getting tired of all the rules in this School. I will have to ask my mother to get me another School where they are less strict.

Vice Principal: All of you move to the front of my office.

[All the late comers move to the front of the V. P's Office]

Vice Principal: We are not interested in punishing you. We want you all to end up being useful and law abiding citizens of this great Nation and be good Ambassadors of this great Institution of learning. I only want to encourage you to come early to School and be good students.

All the Students: Thank you Sir.

[They disperse and leave for their classes]

Teacher:	Why are you just coming in to my class?
Ibukun:	I was at the Vice Principal's Office.
Teacher:	Doing what?
Ibukun:	All the late comers were asked to go there and I was among, we have just been released.
Teacher:	That's Ok and don't be late to School again. *[Pause]* where are your parents?
Ibukun:	At home
Teacher:	Were you not told to invite them this morning?
Ibukun:	I was told.
Teacher:	Why are they not here?
Ibukun:	Is it too late for them to be here?
Teacher:	Are you asking me that question?
Ibukun:	No ma.

Teacher: Who are you asking then?

Ibukun: I don't know ma.

Teacher: I don't think you're ready to continue
                your studies in this School because of all
                the bad behavior of yours.

Ibukun: I thought you will allow my parents to
                be here before passing your judgment
                on me. Do I go home to tell them not to
                bother coming because you're already
                passing your judgments.

Teacher: I just want to advise you to be able to
                make it in life, you have to submit
                yourself to discipline and learn to
                behave decently in the ways and
                manners that are approved of by the
                society.

                [His mother walks in at this point]

Adetutu: Good day Teacher.

Teacher: Good day ma and welcome. Are you
                Ibukun's mother?

Adetutu: Yes I am. I understood you beat him
                mercilessly yesterday, the reason I am
                here to warn you , never I repeat never

to beat him to a pulp like that again. You should have sent for me instead.

Teacher: This is not the best way to approach this issue ma. You should have asked why you were sent for.

Adetutu: Do you mean I should have waited for you to kill him before I talk. No, I won't allow you kill him.

[The Principal is moving from one class to the other to ensure smooth running of the School]

Principal: Mrs. Philips, what's going on here?

Mrs. Philips: Sir, this is the mother of the boy that was asked to invite his parents. She came in Sir without asking why she was sent for and started fomenting trouble.

Principal: Hello madam, what is the matter?

Adetutu: After your teacher has told lies against me, what else do you want to hear from me?

Principal: Do you know the offence your child has committed?

Adetutu: Whatever the magnitude of his offence, could that be a license for you people to have beaten him blue black and still send for his parents; why can't you send for us first before such punishment was meted out to him.

Principal: I can see you are an arrogant woman and you are not giving your child good home training.

Adetutu: Did I ask you to train him for me, and by the way, are you his class teacher, what concerns you in this matter?

Principal: I am the Principal of this School and everyone else here works under me. there's nothing happening in the School I shouldn't know about.

Adetutu: If I may ask, have you invited me for a fight, why are you teaming up with your teacher against me?

Principal: Nobody is fighting you. We have only invited you to explain what your child did and to let you know the steps the School Authority is likely to take.

Adetutu: What other steps can you take that can be more than the one you have taken already. I am here to hear from you why a legal action should not be taken against you for the treatment given my child, having committed no offence against the School. The offence he committed was against another student and not the School.

Principal: Do you know what you are saying at all?

Adetutu: Do I look like a Drunk or an insane person?

Principal: I'm afraid madam; we may have to expel your son from this School if you as a parent, is putting up this kind of attitude.

Adetutu: Is your School the only School in this neighbourhood? If you ask him to leave, then, he goes to another that is even better than yours.

Principal: Thank you ma. You can now leave with your child. We will send you his letter of expulsion from the School later or do you want to collect it now?

Adetutu: Of what relevance is the letter? Keep your letter to yourself.

[Turns to Ibukun]

You go and pack your books; you are leaving the School this minute, I will get you a better one.

[Leaves in annoyance with her son a promise never to return him to the School again]

Don't worry my dear. We will get you a better, I will make sure you don't go to Schools where their teachers and Principals are wicked again just like this your former School.

Ibukun: Thanks ma but what about my sister, is she still going to continue in the School?

Adetutu: Yes she will, since they have not been battering her. The very day they lay a finger on her is the day I will withdraw her too.

Ibukun: That's fine. I trust you, up mom.

[Going home they meet Mrs. Eyitayo; Durojaye's cousin]

Mrs. Eyitayo: Hello my wife.

Adetutu: Good morning and how are you ma?

Mrs. Eyitayo: Better than yesterday, thank you.

Where are both of you coming from at this time of the day?

Adetutu: From his former School.

Mrs. Eyitayo: Has he changed his School, when and why?

Adetutu: Yes, we decided to change his School because the teachers in that School were not treating him well. It was every day they beat him. No one can be beating even an animal like that.

Mrs. Eyitayo: If what you have alleged is true, then that is bad, but did you take the pains to find out what the cause of the matter was? You see sometimes these children might not be telling the whole truth. It is your duty as parents to get to the root of the matter before knowing exactly what step to take.

Adetutu: My son is not a liar. Anything he says is true so, I don't need to search for what is not lost. Those teachers are wicked. They treat other people's chidren poorly as if they had none to call theirs.

Mrs. Eyitayo: Has my cousin taken the pain to visit the School for explanation?

Adetutu: But you know the kind of cousin you have. He's always claiming to be firm and decent and would not want to dabble into matters like this.

Mrs. Eyitayo: Then is it your unilateral decision to take the boy away from that School and to be registered elsewhere?

Adetutu: Who else do I need to consult?

Mrs. Eyitayo: You mean your husband has no hand in all these?

Adetutu: I don't think I need to seek his consent concerning this

Mrs. Eyitayo: My wife, are you not biting more than you can chew these days?

Adetutu: Have I done anything wrong by not allowing one stupid and wicked teacher kill my son. Good or evil, one's child is one's. It is not possible for me to claim another person's child so I have to protect mine.

Mrs. Eyitayo: Anyway, you can go; I will see my cousin in the evening to discuss this matter but you – Ibukun, you're not helping yourself by being arrogant and your mother is not helping you either.

Adetutu: It is my husband that has dragged me on the floor to be trampled upon by all of you if not, what concerns you about my son's affair, are you the one paying his fees, Is anyone asking you to contribute anything – money or material, towards his change of School?

Ibukun: Mummy, that's enough since she has left, you cannot be talking alone otherwise people around may be thinking you're mentally deranged.

Adetutu: Don't worry, the next time she makes any uncomplimentary remarks about my affairs, I will tell her what she's not going to forget in a hurry; that she will know the stuff I'm made of.

[Pulls him by the hand and both leave for home]

ACT THREE SCENE TWO

Mrs. Eyitayo: *[Knocks]* good evening.

Adetutu: Good evening and welcome

Mrs. Eyitayo: Is he at home?

Adetutu: Who?

Mrs. Eyitayo: Your husband of course. Who else do you expect me to be asking of?

Adetutu: He is not the only one living in this house. Anyway, he's in

Mrs. Eyitayo: *[Enters and takes seat]*

Durojaye: Tayo, how are you and your family?

Mrs. Eyitayo: We are fine. How many times will I tell you not to call me Tayo again? I'm already a mother, call me by my daughter's name – Mama Caro or Mama Caroline. I hope I won't have the cause to correct you again on this Sir. *[Laughs]*

Durojaye: I am sorry Tayo, I will adjust.

Mrs. Eyitayo: There you go again, still repeating the same thing, anyway, that's not why I am here.

Durojaye: Hope there's nothing wrong?

Mrs. Eyitayo: God forbid. I saw your wife in the morning with Ibukun returning from School. I was told he has left that School because his teachers always scold him.

Durojaye: This woman called my wife is a big thorn in my flesh. She's a very big hole in my heart causing me pains, I mean pains everyday. Honestly speaking I regret the day I took her for a wife. She is working hard, very hard to destroy the future of that boy. Here in this house, I cannot say a word; before I open my mouth to say one, she must have said five. I'm confused, I don't know how best to handle her case.

Mrs. Eyitayo: What I will suggest is this, she has her life to live buy you must not allow her to ruin the lives of the children because they are your tomorrow.

Durojaye: Thank you. I'll see what can be done about it

Mrs. Eyitayo: Please find time to visit the School tomorrow to know if it's a decision that could be reversed. I know he must have committed an offence after all he's not the only one in the School. Has Shade left the School too?

Durojaye: No. she's still there. She's well behaved but as for her brother, I'm afraid.

Mrs. Eyitayo: Afraid of what?

Durojaye: His future is bleak, I mean very bleak. I understand he moves with boys of questionable characters. You may find it hard to believe that this boy has started taking drugs.

Mrs. Eyitayo: Drugs, what sort of drug is that?

Durojaye: He's already taking Cannabis.

Mrs. Eyitayo: Marijuana you mean?

Durojaye: Yes, Marijuana. I don't know where or how he wants to end his life. One thing is sure, his mother has already ruined him because he doesn't have any good plans for himself. What pains me the most is that he's brilliant, he is naturally talented but for his ways of life, I'm afraid.

Mrs. Eyitayo: You still needed to do everything within your power to rehabilitate him so as not to constitute future menace.

Durojaye: I will try if only his mother will allow me put his feet on the right path again.

Mrs. Eyitayo: She's indeed a very difficult person. I need to know how you're coping with her.

Durojaye: She is a big thorn in my flesh. Some say it is with a lot of perseverance that the thorn can be removed.

Mrs. Eyitayo: Just continue to endure and tolerate her. She may likely change her bad behavior someday.

Durojaye: Which day? Let me tell you that this one cannot change again. She's arrogant and too full of herself. She will not listen to you not to talk of reasoning with you. She thinks everything she does is right.

Mrs. Eyitayo: We will still not give up praying for both of them. There's nothing prayers cannot achieve. Effective prayer of the righteous availeth much says the Holy Book. *[Rises up to take her Sidebag]*

I have to take my leave now.

Durojaye: Thanks for your concern. Blood they say is thicker than water.

Mrs. Eyitayo: Sure.

[They both leave the living room, pass through the main entrance]

***

[Months later, Adetutu starts having Labour pains]

Durojaye: Is anything the matter, why aren't you sleeping by this time of the night?

Adetutu: I don't know exactly what the matter is.

Durojaye: Do you need to bath in case you're feeling hot, to calm you down and then sleep.

Adetutu: No, not that. I am beginning to feel some pains at the lower part of my abdomen.

Durojaye: What is that supposed to mean?

Adetutu: But this is not the first time you will put a woman in the family way. Can't you reason that this Labour pains?

Durojaye: So what do we do?

Adetutu: Are you asking me, don't you know you have to take me to the hospital as early as possible? The pain is becoming severe.

Durojaye: We don't have a Car and there are no night Cabs here. The few Neighbours that have Cars may not listen to me because you have fought all of them.

Adetutu: Look, this is not the time to discuss that. Just go get assistance. If it requires begging please do after all, you know how to prostrate for them to get what you can't provide your family. This is one of such; so, go and sort yourself out because I have to be at the hospital this minute.

Durojaye: Gather your things together while I go seek help.

Adetutu: My things are all ready.

                 [He goes to one of his Neighbours who readily gives assistance.

Alhaji: *[Stops his tahjud to attend to him]* Hope all is well?

Durojaye: It's my wife

Alhaji: *[Now afraid]* What happens?

Durojaye: She's having Labour pains, I needed to take her to the hospital.

Alhaji: How may I be of assistance?

Durojaye: You know I don't have a Car, I want you to please drop us at the hospital.

Alhaji: Allahu Akbar. No problem at all. This is one the reasons we're Neighbours. We must be prepared to come to the aid of our fellow brethren all the time.

* * * * * *

[Shortly after being admitted at the hospital, before the Nurses could compete all the necessary things to do, she started complaining that she wants to visit the rest room and before long, she gives birth to a bouncing baby boy. It's more of precipitate labour]

Nursing Officer: Mr. Durojaye *[She calls]*

Durojaye: Yes ma, I'm here

Nursing Officer: Congratulations. Your wife has given birth to a baby boy.

Durojaye: *[Excited and jumps for joy]* Thank you God. Please can I see them now?

Nursing Officer: Yes Sir. That's why I have come to call you to see your wife and baby and also to take the placenta for proper disposal.

Durojaye: Thank you and God bless.

                        [He enters to see the wife and the baby]

73

Congratulations my dear.

Adetutu: Thank you. I hope you will now stop knocking at my door. It is not easy going through these pains in old age.

Durojaye: Who calls you an old woman?

Adetutu: It's my body that tells me. We have to decide fast on the family planning method to adopt.

Durojaye: Don't worry dear, that is a discussion for another time. Not now and not here.

Adetutu: If you don't discuss hospital issues at the hospital, is it at the Church you want it discussed?

Durojaye: I am sorry. Please don't take offence.

Adetutu: Ok. Since you wish it's postponed then let it be.

Durojaye: How soon are we leaving this place?

Adetutu: That is for the Doctors and the Nurses to determine. We are not paying any additional fee so, don't be afraid of our further stay. Everyone knows it is a lot easier to pull out hairs from the Nostrils than to bring money out from your pockets. Shameless Miser. Your palms have natural adhesives.

Durojaye: I don't deserve all these names you often call me. Heaven knows I always my utmost best to take care of you and your children.

Adetutu: I know your witnesses are the heavens and not the earths. You and I know well that heavens will not come down to testify. Isn't that a clever way of not telling the truth?

Durojaye: All the same, congratulations once again. I think I can leave now to get something for you to eat.

Adetutu: I thought you have done that already. Why are you still here talking about the heavens when food is yet to be ready here on earth.

Durojaye: I will soon be back with the food.

[*As he's about leaving, she calls him again*]

Adetutu: Duro.

Durojaye: Yes, anything the matter?

Adetutu: You must not bring food with much pepper. A little quantity of pepper will do otherwise you will eat the food yourself.

Durojaye: Don't worry. I may not even put pepper at all so as not to incur your wrath.

[He's thinking and soliloquizing as he walks towards the hospital gate. He often says to himself that she's such a big and painful hole in his heart]

Adetutu: Just hurry up. I am famished already. A Nursing mother must eat always, good food of course, to be able to lactate well.

ACT THREE SCENE THREE

[Ibukun couldn't go far in his education, drops out of School to become a street boy while Shade and Adejare are doing well with their studies]

Mr. Fredrick: Adelaja, take this letter and give to your parents at home, tell them I'll see tomorrow Saurday in the morning.

Adelaja: Yes Sir. *[Collects the small white envelope containing a small piece of paper. On getting home, keeps the letter pending the arrival of his father from work]*

Adelaja: Hello Mummy.

Adetutu: You're back, how was School today?

Adelaja: Very fine Mom. Anything to eat?

Adetutu: Won't you remove your uniform and put on something else before asking for food and by the way, were you not given home work today being Friday?

Adelaja: Trust your son Mom. I did my assignment before leaving School because I don't want anything like the Television or something else to distract my attention or prevent me from doing my work at home.

Adetutu: That's my boy.

Adelaja: Mummy, is it true am your boy?

Adetutu: Yes you are, don't you know?

Adelaja: Then how come people point accusing finger at you that you ruined my senior brother's life

Adetutu: Who is the one telling such a stupid story?

Adelaja: No one in particular. I hear it everywhere I go that you spoilt him and that you're the reason Daddy stays out late because you always give a fight over trivial issues.

Adetutu: Don't listen to any of their side talks anymore. Those people talking are not members of this family and frankly speaking, nothing concerns them about our family affairs.

Adelaja: Mummy, you need to be making Daddy happy. He stays out late and drinks heavily too. I learnt he wasn't like this before. Why must you be pushing him to things that are not in his characters?

Adetutu: Don't mind your father, he's merely trying to run away from a problem waiting for him at home; no matter how far and how fast he runs away from home, whenever he returns, he will still meet the problem because it's going nowhere.

Adelaja: Then what exactly do you want him to
do?

Adetutu: I don't know. Ask him anytime he decides to return home.

[Knocks on the door]

Adetutu: Who's at the door please?

Durojaye: It's me

Adetutu: *[Opens the door and he enters]*

You are home early today what happens, did they drive you out of your drinking joint or money has finished in your pocket? I was told Madam Jejelaye use to grant you credit facilities because you're a committed customer.

Durojaye: When will you learn to accord me the respect I deserve as your husband despite the love I have for you.

Adetutu: Respect under my foot. Just tell me, who is that responsible husband you know that returns home the hour the hour you return daily and always drinking himself to stupor as your manner is.

Durojaye: I don't need to tell you before you know that you are the hole in my heart.

Adetutu: *[Laughs]* Sorry o. I didn't know you have a heart not to talk of having a hole in it. I just pray the hole does not send you to your early grave.

Durojaye: *[Goes into his room, sits on his bed and begins to wonder the kind of woman he has for a wife]*

Adelaja: Daddy *[Goes into his father's room and gives him the letter]*

Durojaye: *[Going through the letter]*

Dear sir, with humility I have written this letter to you. I want to ask for your permission to allow your son – Adelaja – to be living with me. Looking at his performances at School, it is obvious that he has the potentials of becoming great in life if he's given the necessary support. I therefore want to contribute my own small quota towards the realization of his success in life. I shall come to pay your family a visit on this important issue tomorrow. Thank you sir and God bless. I remain yours sincerely, K.K. Fredrick.

This is a good report. Who is that parent that will oppose a good plan like this for his child. I am happy for him not taking after his senior brother and mother.

Darling *[He calls]*

Adetutu:	Yes please. What is the matter again this time?

Durojaye:	Go through this letter *[Handing over the letter to her, her countenance changes]*

Adetutu:	What do you want me to do about it?

Durojaye:	I want to solicit your support so that we can allow this boy stay with his teacher for improvements.

Adetutu:	Over my dead body. How can I allow my child to be used as slave in this modern World, Is he an Orphan? How do you think I ever can agree with you to abuse our child?

Durojaye: This case is quite different from the child abuse the government is fighting against. This is about proper development of the boy to be able to make it and faster in life.

Adetutu: How can you allow your child to be living with someone that is not married? Don't you know that such are usually not responsible.

Durojaye: Being married does not signify being responsible in all cases. Some are single and highly responsible while some are married, yet, grossly irresponsible. Ever since we knew K.K, he has always proved to be very responsible and doesn't joke with his job. All the students and his colleagues love him so much. He's paying us a visit tomorrow and I have planned to accede to his request.

Adetutu: That can't be possible. It is better you go to him early tomorrow morning to tell him not to bother coming because we're not granting his request. Let him look for another child to develop, not ours.

Durojaye: Ok. Good night but remember that by tomorrow we shall know who the head of the family is. Do you want this one to also be like Ibukun whose life you have ruined.

Adetutu: Who ruined him? Shameless Drunk. I don't know what gives you the impression that my son's life is ruined.

Durojaye: Thank you. Just go to your room. Like mother like son.

ACT THREE SCENE FOUR

[A gentle knock at the door]:

Adelaja: Goes to open for the visitor] Good morning Sir.

Mr. Fredrick: Good morning my dear and how are you?

Adelaja: I am fine Sir.

Mr. Fredrick: Did you deliver my letter to your Dad yesterday?

Adelaja: Yes I did Sir.

Mr. Fredrick: Is he in?

Adelaja: Yes he is. Have your seat sir while I inform him of your presence.

[He goes to call his father]

Durojaye: Hello K.K. and how are you today?

Mr. Fredrick: Oh better than yesterday Sir

Durojaye: I always love to hear this response of yours that each one of your day is always better than the previous one. My own today too is better than my yesterday and I give God all the glory.

Mr. Fredrick: That's terrific. Sir, I sent a note to you yesterday through your son and I hope he delivers it

Durojaye: Yes he did and I was happy going through the contents.

[Adetutu sashays across the living room to the kitchen and back to her room]

Before we go further let me invite his mother. A bird does not fly with only one wing so goes the saying of our elders. *[He calls his wife to join them]*

Adetutu: Yes please

Durojaye: Please come, we need your attention here

Adetutu: What kind of attention do you need from me?

Durojaye: With respect to the letter sent to us yesterday, K.K. has come to ask us to allow Adelaja to stay with him for more effective learning which will be to the benefit of us all.

Adetutu: And what was my reaction when you informed about this yesterday, did I not tell you that our child is not going to be slave to anyone in his own native land? We hear of people travelling abroad to become slaves even when God has not made them so. They go there to become baby Seaters, housekeepers, bathing corpses just because they want foreign Currencies but in this case what is it you want to achieve by turning your own child to Slave before your very eyes. If it is food or clothing, God will continue to provide so, leave the boy alone. I don't know how many children you have that you cannot take care of.

Durojaye: You got it all wrong. It's neither about food nor clothing, but about a glorious future for our child and all of us. Our prayer has always been for these children to occupy positions of greatness in life and this is one of the sure ways of achieving that.

Mr. Fredrick: Excuse me ma, I am not thinking of taking your child for house help. No, not at all. He has some qualities of greatness in him, he's hardworking and very brilliant. I am encouraged by all these and that is why I pick interest in him. Please allow me give him sound coaching, I know you'll be very proud of him in the near future.

Adetutu: If your intentions are as good as you have painted them then, he's free to stay with you provided he's willing because have not even asked him.

Durojaye: He's happy about it. It is your position that scares him but now that you have consented, there's no problem at all.

[Turns to K.K. Fred.]

How soon do you want him to be with you?

Mr. Fredrick: As soon as you wish Sir. I promise to take very good care of him.

Durojaye: In that case, he will join you next week. We needed to prepare one or two things before he joins you. We like to sew one or two additional clothes for him, buy a travel bag to pack his clothes. I also need to buy him a new Sandal and ……

Mr. Fredrick: He's not travelling out of the Country yet; you don't need to buy everything that comes to your mind. He cannot be living with me without my provisions for him too. Please think less of him while with me. God will help me to do the best for him.

Adetutu: Thank you K.K. Fred. God will provide a good wife for you whenever you wish to choose one. The bone of your bone and the flesh of your flesh is that which God will give you. A wife that will be obedient to you and one that will not in any way be a thorn in your flesh.

Durojaye: Enough of these long prayers of yours. How I wish those who preach Sermons also practice them then the World would be a better place for all.

Mr. Fredrick: Thank you Sir and thank you Ma. I have to leave now.

Durojaye: Thanks so much for this kind gesture. May the good Lord be with you.

Mr. Fredrick: Amen. Bye Adelaja, I'll see you on Monday. [Greets in a way he hears him from his room]

Adelaja: Bye Sir [Answers from his room]

Adetutu: [Peeps to be sure K.K. has left]

Durojaye, when has it become an offence to pray for someone just like I did for K.K.?

Durojaye: No one says it's a crime to pray the way you did. What is wrong is that you don't practice what you seem to be preaching in that lengthy prayer Session.

Adetutu: Are you saying that I give you headache?

Durojaye: No, not just headache but something more severe than ordinary headache, it's the whole body ache.

****

[Two years later]

Mr. Fredrick: Good evening Sir

Durojaye: Good evening dear K.K.

Mr. Fredrick: I have come to inform you Sir that I have been transferred to the city, and that it is with immediate effect. The transfer came with promotion attached. I am now a more senior Tutor.

Durojaye: Congratulations on your promotion. I pray that more and more of it will come your way, just continue to be more assiduous and being kind to everyone. The reward is always there.

Mr. Fredrick: Thanks Sir for your words of encouragements all the time. I shall be leaving for the city with Adelaja Sir. I cannot afford leaving him behind; it is every day he impresses me with his academic performances. I am sure, beyond even the Skies is the limit for him.

Durojaye: Adelaja is yours. You are quite free to take him along with you

Mr. Fredrick: I have just obtained a Scholarship form for him and I am preparing him for the Examination. With his rate of assimilation, success is awaiting him.

Durojaye: I cannot thank you enough for assisting us as much as this. The good Lord will continue to be with you.

Mr. Fredrick: It is getting dark outside I have to leave. My regards to Madam. Good night Sir and bye.

Durojaye: Good night. Extend my greetings to Adelaja.

[After K.K.'s exit, he tries to explain to his wife]

Where are you?

Adetutu: I am in the room. *[She answers from her room]*

I saw you discussing with K.K. , I felt not to intrude, that was why I didn't bother greeting him.

Durojaye: That's thoughtful of you but there was nothing secret we were discussing. He came to inform us of his transfer and that he would go with Adelaja to the city his new place of work.

Adetutu: What did you tell him when he said our son will go with him?

Durojaye: What else do you want me to say knowing he has good plans for the boy.

Adetutu: My goodness. Are you in your right frame of mind, do you know what you're saying at all? Someone you don't know well enough, you don't know any member of his family, I guess you don't even know his hometown. What do you know about him apart from the fact that he works here as a teacher. It is only my Creator that can deliver me from the stupidity of this man called my husband.

Durojaye: I have learnt to develop thick skin to all these senseless talk of yours. You can go ahead to say all that please you, I will not utter a word in response. If we cannot trust and believe fellow human beings, how then are we to believe and trust God we can't see.

Adetutu: *[Moves closer and holds him with his dress]*

You are going to produce my son this minute. He must not sleep in that teacher's house tonight.

Durojaye: For God's sake, let us allow him stay where he is. We shall be made proud at the end and you will be the one to praise K.K. the most for what God must have used him to do in the life of the boy.

******

[K.K. and Adelaja leave for the city]

Mr. Fredrick: Our journey to the city must be seen as an Excursion by you, meaning you must be prepared to write an essay on this journey to the city.

Adelaja: Yes Sir. I have already been thinking along that line.

[At the Motor park are different people heading for different destinations while the Touts are shouting on top of their voices calling on passengers to join vehicles going to their different destinations]

Adelaja: Sir, travelling by Car is very expensive going by what the Conductors are saying, will it not be better we go by Bus?

Mr. Fredrick: Yes 'Laja you're right but it takes longer time for a Bus to be full with passengers. Let's join this Peugeot 505 Car that's almost ready, with us it remains only one more passenger.

****

[Sometimes later in the city, Mr. Fredrick encouraging Adelaja]

Mr. Fredrick: You must not forget all that you have learnt because we don't know the scope of the Examination but I'm sure it won't go beyond what you have studied.

Adelaja: Thank you Sir for all you have been doing for me. I promise not to let you down, not even in this Examination.

Mr. Fredrick: Remember to pray for success and God's favour too. Nothing goes well without prayers.

Adelaja: When exactly is the Examination coming up Sir?

Mr. Fredrick: This Saturday. It is not for students in this State alone but for the entire Country and the over-all best participant will be sent abroad on a Scholarship with a lot other benefits attached.

Adelaja: I have to put in the best in me. God will help me.

Mr. Fredrick: You have always been putting in your best in all that you do. That's a good Spirit, keep it up.

****

[Three days later]

Mr. Fredrick: Adelaja, you ought to have been up by now, what are still doing in bed. Have you forgotten today is your Examination day?

Adelaja: I have been up since, I was saying my prayers as you taught me to have it before leaving bed each morning.

Mr. Fredrick: That's good. You must do quick to get to the venue on time.

Adelaja: Yes Sir.

[Six weeks later, results are released, Adelaja emerges the over-all best followed with a wide margin by a girl from another State]

Mr. Fredrick: I don't know how to express my joy of today. There is no word that can adequately describe how great I feel. I am very proud of you just like I have always been saying and now I have all the reasons to continue saying so.

Adelaja: I too don't know how to thank you enough Sir. You have really established my life. Next to God Almighty is you for me. I can never forget you Sir.

Mr. Fredrick: Let's give God all the glory, thanks and praises. I am going to miss you dearly. In the Newspaper publication that carries the Results of the Examination, It is indicated that the process of obtaining your Visa will commence almost immediately. We have to go to the Headquarters to get the details and to fill all the necessary forms in preparation for your journey. When you get there, please don't forget to still face your studies very well. You could still get another Scholarship if you continue to work hard and I am sure a very good job awaits you after leaving School.

Adelaja: Sir, when do you hope to inform my parents about this development? I know my father will be so excited to hear this.

Mr. Fredrick: Without asking, I have planned that we will travel home this weekend to visit your parents. I will return that same day while you can stay for one or two days with them.

Adelaja: I'll be happy to see my parents again after all these while.

ACT THREE SCENE FIVE

[Mr. Fredrick and Adelaja leave the city early in the morning of Saturday for town. Approaching Durojaye's Compound, they notice an unusually large number of people thinking Mummy and Daddy are doing the usual thing]

Neighbour 1: You just have to behave like a man. No amount of tears can bring him back even if you're to cry from now till eternity. Just accept it as an act of God.

Durojaye: What else can anyone do about it? It has happened and that's all. I warned his mother several times but she would not listen, she would rather indulge him the more. Now she's accusing me of throwing away our second son – Adelaja.

Neighbour 1: So how's Adelaja?

Durojaye: I have not heard anything about him since they left for the city but I believe all is well with them. I don't have their address and they have sent us any mail.

Neighbour 2: God will give you fortitude to bear this irreparable loss. It is not an easy thing to lose a grown up child with the son's where about unknown.

Where is their mother?

Durojaye: She has been taken to the next Compound because she has been weeping bitterly and would not be consoled.

[Mr. Fredrick and Adelaja entered]

Adelaja: Daddy, what's the matter, why is everyone looking sad, what happens to my mother?

Durojaye: My good Son, you're welcome. How are you and K.K.?

Adelaja: We came together, what is the matter?

Durojaye: We lost Ibukun your brother.

Adelaja: *[Shouts and falls down but he's quickly assisted by the sympathizers]*

How did it happen?

Durojaye: You all knew he was a spoilt child. He joined a bad gang and you know that bad company corrupts good manners. His Cult group went for the initiation of their new members, the Security Agents were alerted and swooped on them, in his attempt escape arrest, he fell as a result of gunshot and died. His remains has just been buried.

Adelaja: Where is Mummy?

Neighbour 3: She is the next Compound

[Adelaja in the next Compound]

Ponle: Adetutu here comes your Son. The person to stop you from crying and hurting yourself has now come.

Adelaja: Mummy, sorry for what has happened to my brother. You have to take heart because no amount of tears rolling down your cheeks can bring back the dead. Please ma put yourself together. No Evil will befall us again.

[All chorus Amen]

Adetutu: How is K.K.?

Adelaja: He's fine, we came together.

Adetutu: How did you get to hear about this?

Adelaja: We didn't hear any news before leaving the city. Let's go back to our house and be with Daddy, I have a very good news for the family.

[His mother quickly gets up and follows him]

Mr. Fredrick: Sorry for what happened ma. There won' be a re-occurrence of this Evil I pray.

Adetutu: Thank you and thanks for taking good care of Adelaja.

Adelaja: Where is Shade?

Durojaye: She has gained admission to The Polytechnic and she's in School. She has not heard of her brother's demise.

Mr. Fredrick: With situation of things, I won't be able to stay long. We have very good news for you and the news is that your Son *[pointing to Adelaja]* participated in a competition and came first and has since been given Scholarship to study abroad and will be leaving the Country soon.

[Durojaye jumps up in ecstasy and shouted P-r-a-i-s-e God while Adetutu was dumbfounded with both of them shedding tears of joy]

Durojaye: What can I say or do that can compensate you for what you have done for us in this family. On this day of mourning, you brought us great joy; you give light to replace our darkness, you turned our sadness to overwhelming joy and happiness. How are we to thank you enough.

Mr. Fredrick: Let us return all the glory to God Almighty.

THE END

Glossary

Allahu Akbar   -   Allah is the greatest

Papa Ibk   -   Ibk's father

Tahjud   -   Muslim's night prayer